PLANETA ANIMAL

SEALS

BY CHRISTOPHER BAHN

CREATIVE EDUCATION • CREATIVE PAPERBACKS

Published by Creative Education and Creative Paperbacks
P.O. Box 227, Mankato, Minnesota 56002
Creative Education and Creative Paperbacks
are imprints of The Creative Company
www.thecreativecompany.us

Design by The Design Lab
Art direction by Graham Morgan
Edited by Jill Kalz

Images by flickr/Biodiversity Heritage Library, 8, 22–23; Getty Images/Douglas Klug, 5, George Karbus Photography, 13, Ian_Sherriffs, 18, Paul Souders, 14; Pexels/Niklas Jeromin, 16; Unsplash/Anchor Lee, 9, karlheinz_eckhardt Eckhardt, 6, Keith Luke, 21, Neil Cooper, 7; Wikimedia Commons/Andreas Trepte, 10, AWeith, 2, Magnus Johansson, 1, Mike Baird, 17, Piotrus, 20

Library of Congress Cataloging-in-Publication Data
Names: Bahn, Christopher (Children's story writer), author.
Title: Seals / by Christopher Bahn.
Description: Mankato, Minnesota : Creative Education and Creative Paperbacks, [2025] | Series: Amazing animals | Includes bibliographical references and index. | Audience: Ages 6–9 | Audience: Grades 2–3 | Summary: "Discover the deep-sea-diving seal! Explore the marine mammal's anatomy, diet, ocean habitat, and life cycle. Captions, on-page definitions, a Celtic animal story, additional resources, and an index support elementary-aged kids"—Provided by publisher.
Identifiers: LCCN 2024011055 (print) | LCCN 2024011056 (ebook) | ISBN 9798889892489 (library binding) | ISBN 9781682776148 (paperback) | ISBN 9798889893592 (ebook)
Subjects: LCSH: Seals (Animals)—Juvenile literature. | Seals (Animals)—Behavior—Juvenile literature. | Seals (Animals)—Life cycles—Juvenile literature.
Classification: LCC QL737.P64 B34 2025 (print) | LCC QL737.P64 (ebook) | DDC 599.7915—dc23/eng/20240415
LC record available at https://lccn.loc.gov/2024011055
LC ebook record available at https://lccn.loc.gov/2024011056

Printed in China

Table of Contents

Common harbor seals live in the Pacific and Atlantic oceans.

Seals are sleek marine animals. They are excellent swimmers and divers. Seals belong to a group of animals called pinnipeds. Other pinnipeds are walruses and sea lions. There are about 30 kinds of seal. They live all around the world.

marine of the sea

Seals rest on rocks to warm up, relax, and spend time with other seals.

Seals live in warm and cold water. Most of them live around the North and South poles. They are well adapted to cold ocean water. Blubber and fur keep them warm.

adapted changed to improve the chances of survival

blubber a thick layer of fat under the skin of some marine animals

Seals come in many sizes. Ringed seals are small. On average, they weigh 100 pounds (45 kilograms). Southern elephant seals are the biggest. Males may be nearly 20 feet (6.1 meters) long and weigh more than 8,000 pounds (3,629 kg).

Named for the land animals, elephant seals have an especially large nose.

Seal colors range from white to brownish-black.

Seals have front and back flippers. Flippers make seals awkward on land. However, in the water, they help seals swim fast. Seals can make quick, sharp turns. Their smooth, rounded shape helps them shoot through the water.

flippers limbs that are wide and flat like paddles

Deep diving is something seals do well. Some seals can dive 2,000 feet (610 m). They may stay underwater for an hour. Their large, round eyes are good at seeing in dark, deep water.

Some seals swim so fast that they can shoot high into the air and land on floating ice.

Seals are meat eaters. They feed on fish. They also eat hard-shelled animals such as clams. Many seals have cone-shaped teeth. Leopard seals have long sharp teeth like sharks. They hunt penguins and other seals.

A leopard seal's teeth are made for cutting and tearing meat.

Many seals live alone or in small groups most of the year. They travel long distances in the sea to find food. All return to land to have their young. Some seals gather in huge groups called rookeries.

Rookeries can be huge, with tens of thousands of animals on the beach together.

Seal pups may look helpless, but they have a sharp bite.

Baby seals are called pups. Mothers usually give birth to only one pup at a time. Like all mammals, they feed their young milk. After four to six weeks, the pups are old enough to catch fish on their own.

mammals animals with fur or hair that give birth to live young and feed them milk

Seals are playful and smart. Humans have trained them to do many things. Seals do tricks in zoos. They perform in movies and TV shows. They even help with searches for the U.S. Navy.

A seal's best home is in ocean waters.

A *Seal Tale*

Selkies are magical sea creatures that can change their shape. They are like mermaids. The people of Ireland and Scotland have many old stories about them. Selkies often change from seals to humans by taking off their skin. They sometimes fall in love with humans, but their hearts belong to the sea.

Index